Trau ned
Youth Work

Joy Wright
Emerge Advocacy Founder and CEO

GROVE BOOKS LIMITED
RIDLEY HALL RD CAMBRIDGE CB3 9HU

Contents

1 Introduction 3

2 What Do You Mean, 'Trauma-informed'? 5

3 A Theological Perspective 9

4 Trauma-informed Youth Work 12

5 Informed and Credible 16

6 Informed and Equipped 22

Notes 28

Acknowledgments

Thank you to the wonderful Rachel for her guidance and support in the writing of this booklet; it has genuinely been fun! Thank you, too, to my colleagues at Emerge who have allowed me to bounce ideas off them and who set such an amazing example of working with vulnerable young people in a trauma-informed way with so much love, compassion and creativity.

First Impression December 2024
ISSN 1748-3492
ISBN 978 1 78827 437 1

1 Introduction

Have you ever had an experience where you felt a sense of reassurance when speaking with someone you did not know? Perhaps you were at a medical appointment or a meeting where you were apprehensive, but there was just something in their manner, the way they held themselves, or the way they spoke or looked at you which told you that you were in safe hands.

Conversely, you might have had an experience where you were feeling fine in yourself and then you had a conversation or encounter with someone which, on the face of it, seemed perfectly normal, but you noticed a sense of discomfort within yourself during it, or after you left them which you could not explain.

The reason for this is that our bodies and brains are wonderfully complex, and intricately designed to do a multitude of things we are not even aware of. In the same way that we breathe, digest food and circulate blood without having to think about it, our bodies carry out many unnoticed processes as we go about our daily lives, always working to keep us safe and healthy while we are busy wondering what to watch on TV later or waiting to cross the road.

Our bodies carry out many unnoticed processes as we go about our daily lives

Did you know that your body and brain work together to scan your environment and interactions continuously for cues of safety or danger and adapt accordingly? Did you know that those cues, those senses of safety and danger are 'infectious' between people? Did you know that you can enable someone else to feel safe simply by being with them and being calm and well in yourself?

You probably do know this because you will have experienced it, but do you know how it works or why it happens? This is what I am so excited to unpack!

Our understanding of neuroscience and how we as people navigate the world is growing. This is emerging in practice into concepts like trauma-informed care, which you may have heard of. I am not a neuroscientist, but I have found learning about this so inspiring and helpful as a Christian youth worker. There are many connections between the theory of trauma-informed care and the worlds of youth work and theology; in this booklet I will do my best to lay out the basics and to draw some comparisons which I believe can give us new ways to talk about the impact of youth work.

I believe this can increase our confidence in what we do as youth workers when speaking to others, helping us understand a little more about how God created us, as well as how he can use us to come alongside and help one another in the most beautiful ways. It is not a whole new way of working, but rather a fresh insight into what we already do as youth workers and an invitation to grow.

So, let us get into it. First, a bit of science!

What Do You Mean, 'Trauma-informed'?

2

Research has been done for over forty years on trauma and the autonomic nervous system (how our bodies and brains work). It is called autonomic because it does things automatically, without us needing to think about them.

There are three pathways within our autonomic nervous systems:

Connection—where we ideally spend most of our time
We are going about our lives and there are no issues, we are able to think clearly, chat, laugh, concentrate and generally feel like a well-functioning human.

Action—our 'fight' or 'flight' response
We encounter a threat, immediately feeling anxious about our safety. Our nervous system is already in action, boosting our adrenaline in case we need to move quickly, increasing our heart rate and slowing digestion so that all our energy is readily available to help keep us safe. We might feel angry, afraid, or both and we can either stand up for ourselves (fight), or run for the hills (flight).

Shutdown—our 'freeze' or 'flop' response
If fight and flight do not work, we give up. Giving up can look like resigning ourselves to going along with whatever is about to happen or zoning out emotionally. We 'disappear' and feel like all the life, energy and hope has left.

These three pathways form the Polyvagal Defence Hierarchy, and we move between them.[1] The action and shutdown pathways are described as states of emotional dysregulation, while connection is a state of regulation.

Emotional Regulation

Deb Dana talks about neuroception, or perception done directly by our nervous system.[2] Our nervous systems are broadcasting our state of regulation at an autonomic level. We are not trying to do it, and we are not aware that others are doing it, but it is happening. This means that if I am feeling frustrated or anxious, you will get a sense of this (through neuroception) before you have had time to read my body language or notice that my tone of voice seems off.

Your nervous system will have sensed what is going on in mine just by being nearby. How incredible is that?!

What is even more wonderful is that, if you are in a regulated state—relaxed, feeling safe and ready to engage with me—then my nervous system picks up on your vibes of safety through neuroception, and will start calming down. Without saying anything, you can help me start to feel safe, and to come back into a regulated state where I can relate to you, I can start to think clearly, and I can face whatever is troubling me. This is called co-regulation.

If, however, your nervous system picks up my anxiety and you start thinking 'Oh dear, something is wrong, what's the matter with me?' then my dysregulation has triggered you into a dysregulated state too. Then we are both struggling, and you will not even know why—you will be thinking, 'I felt fine a minute ago, what happened?!'

Fascinatingly, however, we can interact with our autonomic nervous system, or 'befriend it,' as Dana says. We can tune in and notice these kinds of shifts and changes, starting to recognize when we are moving towards dysregulation. We can discern whether there is, in fact, a problem going on for us, or whether we are sensing someone else's anxiety or anger, or even if we are reacting to past memories of danger.

We can tune in and start to recognize when we are moving towards dysregulation

Polyvagal theory tells us that a person in a place of emotional safety (regulation) can help someone in distress (dysregulation) to regain regulation through attentive social interaction, building trusting relationships and providing cues of safety which are picked up at an autonomic level. Co-regulation happens through neuroception, when psychological and emotional safety are 'caught' and transferred through being in the physical and emotional presence of someone who is embodying safety.[3]

How Do We Do Co-Regulation?

Co-regulation means helping another person to come out of dysregulation and into regulation, and it has three parts.

First, we build a warm, responsive *relationship*, enabling the other person to know that we care about them, that we are interested in them, and that we are a safe person who is there to help them. This is communicated not only at an autonomic level, but also in our body language, eye contact, what we say and how we say it.

Secondly, we structure the *environment*, helping the person feel oriented in what is currently happening. Imagine a young person arriving at your church youth club for the first time. They were invited by a mate who is not there yet and have never been in the building before, so they loiter by the main entrance without looking directly at anyone. They are worried because they do not have any money with them, and on the way here they lost the form their mum signed. They do not actually know what the club is like—will they be made to say a weird prayer, or be asked awkward questions about God? They are not sure they want to be there, and they are dying for their friend to arrive and rescue them! You go over, smile and introduce yourself. You notice something about their trainers/t-shirt/hair and make a bit of a connection with them. You invite them to the café area, explaining what the club is, and what will be happening that evening. You offer them a drink (on the house) and they start to loosen up a bit. You suggest something they can do while they wait for their friend, and they settle into the activity, nodding to another young person nearby.

It is not youth-work rocket science, but what you just did there was helping that young person to regulate by building a little rapport, helping them get a feel for what is about to happen, and giving them something they can do to help them feel more relaxed.

Finally, in co-regulation, we *coach* self-regulation skills, so we help the person work out what they need to regain a sense of emotional safety and regulation, and what could help them in the future when we are no longer there. What helps each person self-regulate will be as unique as they are, so we need to be mindful not to presume that what works for us will work for them, or that things from books, training or social media will be helpful. They might be, but the important thing is really to listen, helping the person explore options to find things that fit their individual needs.

Understanding how our autonomic nervous systems and co-regulation work underpins the theory of trauma-informed care, which is becoming increasingly mainstream. The NHS, emergency services, schools, charities and other organizations are all beginning to train their staff to become more trauma informed in the way they work.

What is Trauma?

It is important to understand that while trauma can occur from one big event like a war or a terrible accident, it can also arise from a series of smaller and seemingly less significant events or circumstances. For example, living in a family where a parent might often have angry outbursts directed at another family member. A person might experience PTSD as a result, but might not understand why, since the outbursts were not directed at them, and they were never in physical danger. They may even have had siblings who shared the experience but were not particularly affected. It all depends on whether what happened triggered the person onto their action or shutdown pathway, how much, for how long, how frequently, and whether anyone was there to help them regulate and return to their connection pathway, or if they felt alone.

In this way, 'Trauma is not what happens to you, it is what happens inside of you as a result of what happens to you.'[4]

How Does Trauma Affect People?

Since we are all unique, no two people experience the effects of trauma in the same way. It can result in behaviour which may surprise others, for example, seeming rude, disproportional, lazy or unresponsive. The thing to remember is that it is a normal response and is actually our body and brain trying to protect us. The trouble is that we may not be in danger at that time, but our body and brain are reacting as though we were—something has triggered us.

Going back to the Polyvagal Defence Hierarchy and our three pathways, when we hear a noise, smell a smell or encounter a situation that reminds us of the traumatic event, we might jump into the pathway of action or shutdown even if, in the here and now, we are safe. This is not something that we do on purpose—our autonomic nervous system is always automatically scanning for safety and danger, picking up on things that were previously cues for serious danger. Then our defence mechanisms kick in, and before we know it we are in fight, flight or shutdown. We need to find our way back to a state of regulation—to our pathway of connection.

The positive side of neuroception is that we are wired to help one another, because the sense of safety you are experiencing can signal to my nervous system that things are actually okay. And through our abilities as humans to connect and relate, we can intentionally invite one another into that sense of safety through co-regulation.

As Deb Dana says, 'It is in the experience of finding our way to being anchored in…safety and offering that welcome to others that we begin to change the world, one nervous system at a time.'[5]

A Theological Perspective

3

Light and Darkness

The heart of this chapter is the compelling, hope-filled truth that in Jesus, God came to be one of us, to enter into our reality, making a way for us to be in relationship with him. Jesus did not become one of us in order to leave us as we were; he made a way for us to be transformed—to become like him.[6]

John chapter one illuminates the incredible impact of Christ in the world, and in our hearts. He is the life-bringer, the light-bringer. His light shines in the darkness, and the darkness can never extinguish it (John 1.4–5). This truth was known and prophesied even before Christ: 'The darkness is not dark to you; the night is as bright as the day' (Ps 139.12).

There is a lot of darkness in the world young people inhabit. A dip into social media or a school lunch break can trigger comparison, fear, shame, loneliness and identity confusion. The NHS is struggling to keep up with the demands for support coming from the multitude of young people feeling the effects of the darkness in their daily lives.[7]

Jesus came and entered into our despair, sickness, sin and trauma. He became one of us, yet he was without sin. He came into the darkness, but the darkness did not go into him. Because his light shines in the darkness, and the darkness cannot overcome it. No darkness can overcome Jesus' light.[8]

As Christians, Jesus lives in us by his Holy Spirit. This means that the darkness experienced by young people can be displaced by Jesus' light—because he lives in us, for the very purpose of transforming his world with his love.

Releasing Healing

John Swinton describes a confused, frightened young man who was perceived by his family and by professionals as 'uncooperative, hostile and paranoid.' Swinton describes the impact of Blise, whose 'empathetic understanding of his situation enabled her to enter into his situation.' This 'is a *form of understanding that in itself initiates a degree of healing,*' says Swinton, '...it is an attitude that seeks to enter into the experience of people with mental health problems and in so doing focus on ways in which that experience can be understood rather than simply explained.' In this way, 'Blise began to reconnect [this young man] to the human community and to draw him back to a position where the possibility of meaningful relationship and *a revised future (hope) became real.*'[9]

This means that a person can enter into the mess and pain of another and, in doing so, release a measure of healing through their connection, which sounds like what John describes Jesus doing. It also sounds like what Deb Dana says co-regulation can do. What is going on here?

According to Dawna Da Silva, the word 'shine' used to describe Christ's light in Eph 5.11–14 is *epiphausei,* which means 'to shine upon or give light to.' She writes, 'As followers of Christ, we have a mandate to…shine in such a way that we draw people to the one true God. We should be walking transmitters of his character and release his attributes into every atmosphere we encounter.'[10] Da Silva suggests that, where we encounter darkness, we pray and release light. For example, we sense anxiety and we pray, 'I will not partner with fear…I invite you, Holy Spirit, to come and release your peace in this place.'[11] This means we are not rocked by what we perceive, but can instead be a vessel of peace and restoration.

Different Languages, One Reality

On the one hand, there is an unseen, spiritual reality that we broadcast; in Da Silva's words it is the light, hope, freedom, peace and love of Jesus who lives in us. On the other hand, neuroscientists have discovered that a neuroception (unseen sense) of safety and danger can be passed between two people who are in physical proximity to each other, and through relational connection.

I would venture that these are two ways of describing the same thing—the amazing way that God has designed our brains and bodies. It is in these bodies that the spiritual, unseen reality meets the tangible, felt and seen reality.

In Christian language we are 'shifting spiritual atmospheres' because the light shines in the darkness, and in scientific language, 'Other nervous systems feel the energy of safety we are sending and receive an invitation to come into connection.'[12]

Youth Workers as Light-bringers

When we bring all this together as youth workers, there is the potential for exponential impact in the lives of young people.

Youth workers do great co-regulation because we:

- Are skilled in fostering relational connection with young people
- Understand informal education and how to structure the environment for young people

- Instinctively empower and coach young people to learn new skills, coping strategies and techniques to overcome their struggles

Youth workers are naturally trauma informed because we:

- Work in ways that build safety, trust and openness
- Are empowering and collaborative
- Are non-judgmental and break down stereotypes

Christian youth workers do all this in partnership with the Holy Spirit and, together, we:

- Embody unexplainable peace which can be caught
- Have spiritual insight and discernment to perceive how to bring light
- Carry unstoppable love, grace and hope

In Exod 33.15–16, Moses and God are having a conversation. God tells Moses to lead the people into the promised land, but that he will not go with them because of the people's sin. Moses replies to God:

> If your presence does not go with us, do not send us up from here. How will anyone know that you are pleased with me and with your people unless you go with us? What else will distinguish me and your people from all the other people on the face of the earth?

As a Christian youth worker, have you had a situation where you have been able to get through to a young person when no one else has, or perhaps in school a teacher has commented on how a student is so much more peaceful after their mentoring session with you? During COVID-19, a young person who one of my team supported said this: 'I don't know why, but as soon as they came into the room I started to feel calmer. Even though they were wearing a mask I could tell they were smiling and I really felt different.'

God is amazing, and he has created our bodies and brains so wonderfully. We can bring healing and hope to someone else just through sitting down beside them as a person who is operating out of a personal sense of peace. Everyone can do that—by God's grace it is the way he has wired us. But when we consciously partner with him, his presence makes a world of difference because Jesus is the light of the world and he lives in us. We, too, embody his light. This is what 'distinguishes us from all the other people on the face of the earth.'

The light of Jesus shines through us into the darkness, and the darkness cannot overcome it.

4 Trauma-informed Youth Work

This chapter draws out the synergy between trauma-informed practice and youth-work principles and practices, informed by the theological understanding that we have just explored.

Youth Work as Relationship

Relationship is at the heart of youth work. Youth workers get to know young people and allow young people to know them—it is a two-way street. Other professions have different boundaries in this respect; where nurses, police officers and social workers will find out lots of information about a young person in the course of their duties, the young person will learn relatively little about them. Furthermore, the information many other professionals learn about young people is task-oriented, as well as being time-limited and taking place in official environments. As a result, this type of relationship does not often allow for knowing young people as people.

In youth work, however, as Graham Bright reflects, 'The starting point and fundamental vehicle for practice is the youth worker's relationship with young people.'[13] Jeffs and Smith agree that youth work utilizes 'everydayness' in order to intentionally and critically foster learning, raise aspirations, challenge oppression and fulfil potential through engaging, fun, associative, inclusive and democratic practices that enable young people more fully to 'relate to themselves, others and the world.'[14]

So, youth work is less about an intervention and more about a relationship based in the normal, everyday life of the young person and the youth worker, where a genuine relational connection and bond is formed. One could say that youth worker and young person are 'at home' with one another, echoing the words of John 1 describing Christ's coming to dwell with us.

Youth-work Principles and Practices

From this foundation of relationship, we can further understand the nature of youth work as having four cornerstones or principles, which are: participation, equality, education and empowerment. These are described on the National Youth Agency's website: (definitions paraphrased)[15]

Participation:

- Supporting young people to become partners and leaders in their development
- Enabling them to gain influence over issues they are concerned about

Equality:

- Opportunities are open to all young people
- Respecting differences
- Building connections between different groups and demographics

Empowerment:

- Helping young people develop the skills and confidence needed to make decisions and to act; to have a voice

Education:

- Helping young people learn about themselves, others and how to engage in society through informal educational methods

As I learned about trauma-informed care from clinical professionals, what struck me was how closely aligned its principles are with those of youth work. These principles were being taught as something new, as an emerging approach in working with vulnerable people—yet youth workers (among others) have been doing this for years, both instinctively and implicitly. What we have been doing all along is now being recognized and recommended *clinically* as the most effective way to support and help others. Youth work gets it!

Youth Work and Trauma-informed Care

Let us break this down to see how trauma-informed practice and youth work align, unpacking the synergy between them.

Safety

This is about enabling people to feel and be safe in all senses: physically, psychologically, emotionally and spiritually. According to trauma-informed care, the primary way that people experience safety is through relational connection, which is the bedrock of youth work. Therefore, youth workers' natural way of creating trusting and mutual relationships means that young people are helped to feel safe. As a result, youth workers get to know what risks might exist for young people in their lives through observation and because young people will tell us quite honestly about what is going on for them. Youth work creates safe relationships and environments, promoting safety in the rest of a young person's life. This reduces the risks of further trauma, creating a cycle of increasing safety.

Trustworthiness and Transparency

Safe relationships lead to trust, which makes transparency possible. In the context of trusting relationships, young people will be transparent with us about their lives, but it is also important that we are transparent with them about the decisions we make as youth workers which affect them. This connects to the value placed on participation in youth work where, for example, young people become part of the planning of activities and shaping the culture of a group. There is no 'us and them' in youth work. We all have agency and are genuinely known and seen: our presence makes a difference to the rest of the community.

Peer Support

In youth work, young people join a supportive community with those in their age group. In contrast to many other settings where young people mix with peers in a task-focused environment where friendships are a secondary matter, the building of friendships amongst young people is high on the agenda here.

In a trauma-informed framework, the people who benefit from services or activities are part of the planning and delivery of them. Whilst this may be new in clinical settings, this is standard youth-work practice, building on the cornerstone of participation. We take an empowering approach, encouraging young people to be involved in shaping our programmes. We give them opportunities to lead in a safe environment where we set them up for success and enable them to feel supported and able to learn from any mistakes they make.

Collaboration and Mutuality

This is built on the cornerstone of equality, as we learn to recognize and level power differentials. Where one person or group of people might hold more power than others, this is spotted and addressed. For example, amongst young people there may be some who are particularly influential or disadvantaged because of who their parents are within the community—perhaps they are leaders, or perhaps they are looked down upon. Maybe there is a culture of putting a youth or worship leader on a pedestal. Rather than colluding with these spoken or unspoken norms, we work in ways that disrupt them. We model mutuality, running activities that are intended to level the playing field, which, in turn, fosters a supportive environment.

Empowerment, Voice and Choice

A traditional medical model is deficit-based, in that professionals diagnose what is wrong with a person and then act to remedy it using medicine, surgery or therapy. Youth workers, however, are naturally asset-based in approach, seeing the strengths and capabilities of a person and empowering them to build on these. We listen to what is important to young people, trusting that they are the experts on their own lives. We help young people access and take hold of what they need, focusing on grassroots level changes rather than taking a top-down approach. Empowerment, voice and choice are foundational youth-work principles.

Cultural, Historical and Gender

This connects with the cornerstones of education and equality in that well-informed youth workers help young people to become better informed about society, their part within it, and the importance of diversity. This means that biases and stereotypes can be recognized and addressed. Christian youth work is about serving as Jesus did, prioritizing those whom society often rejects, challenging oppression and enabling the marginalized to come into community. As youth workers, for example, if we are working in an area where there are two rival secondary schools, we might purposely structure activities in our youth club to mix young people up and break down barriers, enabling them to overcome their preconceptions about one another.

5 Informed and Credible

As I hope you are coming to see and feel, youth work is awesome—you are awesome, and the way you work is now being recognized and recommended by psychologists and neuroscientists. Doctors, nurses, police officers, paramedics, teachers, prison officers and many other professions are being trained to engage in ways that come naturally to youth workers.

Obviously, the remits and boundaries of each profession vary—a doctor would not be expected to play football with their patients, or a police officer to have regular coffees with a young person. But rather than being about the methods, this is about the principles behind them being recognized as the five-star foundation for working with vulnerable people.

It is also about working together—about recognizing that it takes a range of people to help and support young people who are struggling. It is about dismantling silo-working and getting on the same page, the same team with people from different professions and different parts of the community.

However, in order to work effectively with other professionals, we must present ourselves as credible collaborators.

Curbing the Credibility Killer

In order to unpack this, we will use Karpman's Drama Triangle and its antidote, the Empowerment Triangle, as tools to understand why youth workers can struggle to find a credible voice in this space, and what we can do about it.[16] I have adapted Karpman's models to this context (opposite).

In this drama triangle, the young person is in the role of victim, where they feel powerless and 'done to' by others in their life. This is common within a medical model, as described in the last chapter, where intervention is understood as coming from the professional (the authority figure) to the person in need, with an absence of relationship or shared learning. This often leads to the young person feeling that their social worker, doctor, teacher, parent, mental-health worker—whoever is in a position of authority—is the villain. This means they do not want to listen to them or take their advice (which may actually be quite good) and there is a tendency towards conflict between them. Enter the empathetic and caring youth worker who has a big heart and wants to help the poor young person who is so misjudged and misunderstood by

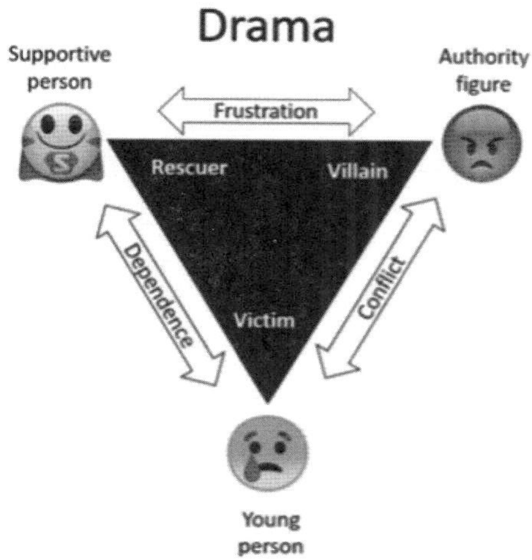

all the other adults in their life. The young person will naturally cling to their youth worker, who is the rescuer in Karpman's model. This sets up a dynamic of dependence between them, with the young person perhaps articulating things like, 'You're the only person who understands me and who I can trust.' Rather than truly helping the young person, we can unintentionally disempower them further by perpetuating the sense that they need us in order to be okay. This is also bad news for our own well-being, as it can lead to burn out if we can never switch off from the young person's needs.

This dynamic also sets us up for conflict with the other adults who are trying to help the young person, as we are influenced by the young person's view of them and become defensive. We feel we must protect the young person—be on their side. The person in the position of authority will experience our presence as hindering the work they are trying to do with the young person and they will likely experience frustration and seek to exclude us from professional conversations. They may also, understandably, dismiss our perspective on the young person's situation, which is sad because we really know this young person and could offer helpful insights, if only we could untangle all the complicated and unhelpful dynamics of the drama triangle.

Thankfully, Karpman's model does not leave us stuck here; he offers the Empowerment Triangle as an alternative. But before we explore this, let me say that we have all been in drama triangles—it happens really easily, and it does not mean we are rubbish. It happens because we care, but it is an indication that we need to stop and think, to reconsider how we are responding. We cannot change how other people respond, but we can make a difference by refusing to add to the drama dynamic, and beginning to act out of an empowerment mindset instead. Let us not forget that empowerment is a cornerstone of youth work, a key principle of trauma-informed care, and a thoroughly Jesus-like way of working.

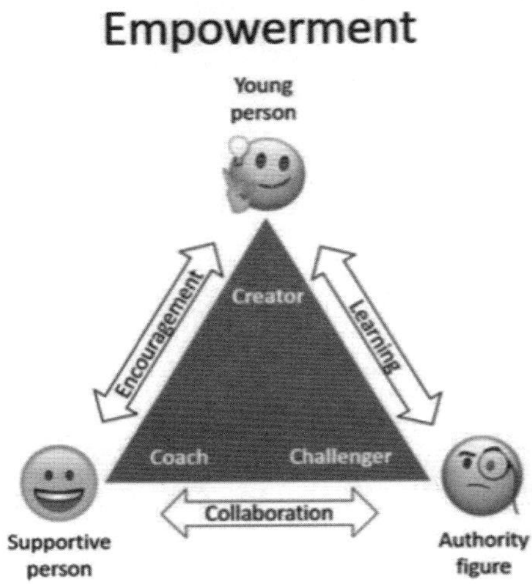

The first change we notice in the Empowerment Dynamic is that the triangle has been turned upside down and the young person is now at the top. They are called the 'creator' because they have the power to make things happen, to make choices, to direct the ship of their life. The authority figure becomes the 'challenger,' using their knowledge and expertise to serve the young person, facilitating through asking questions, and seeking to understand how their knowledge can be best applied to the young person's unique situation. Strategies and plans can be tried and honed through shared learning, rather than a 'one size fits all' approach.

The supportive person, aka the youth worker, becomes the coach, which means they run alongside the young person, encouraging them, cheering them on and helping them to put into practice what they are learning from the challenger. Crucially, we do not do it for them. This opens the way for collaboration between the coach and the challenger, to be working together for the best outcome for the young person, each with different roles but aligned with one another. The responsibility for the young person's progress now lies with the young person themselves, with the support of their youth worker and other adults in their life, but they are not dependent. This is great news for everyone's well-being!

When youth workers understand this, we do ourselves huge favours in terms of being a credible partner to other professionals in the lives of vulnerable young people.

Curating Credibility

We cannot control how others respond but we can control what we say and do. From a place of being secure in our own identity, as a person and a child of God, and in being clear about the scope and boundaries of our role as a youth worker, we can begin to weave this new mindset through our conversations and interactions with others, diverting away from drama and towards empowerment. For example…

Victim/Rescuer to Creator/Coach

If we notice that a young person is responding to us with a sense of dependence, we can gently address this, affirming that we are there to walk alongside them, pointing out their strengths and how far they have come. We can remind them that our role is to help them identify and lay hold of what they need to move forwards, but that they are the ones who will do it for themselves. A young person might say something like, 'I'm so done with speaking to my mental-health worker, they don't understand me or listen, they just tell me what to do and it's so awkward, I can't open up to them like I can with you.' We must resist the temptation to feel flattered, and instead say something like, 'I know it can be hard but remember, there was a time when you and I didn't know each other and it wouldn't have been easy to have deep chats, but you did it with me which means I know you can do it with them too, it just takes time. How about we write some bullet points together so that next time you see them you have something to help you remember what you want to say?'

In this way, we are facilitating and encouraging the growth of the young person's relationship with the other professional—rather than reinforcing the young person's victim mentality, we are putting the ball back in their court and giving them tools to help them succeed. In youth-work language, we are empowering the young person to participate in their care. In the language of trauma-informed care, from a basis of safety and trustworthiness, we are providing support and advocating for collaboration and mutuality, which leads to empowerment of the young person's voice and choices.

Our interactions with young people and the way we respond to them can have a big impact on the way they interact with other professionals, and it is our role to set them up for success. When we recognize and refuse to partner with the drama, we become a credible professional colleague in the multidisciplinary space of mental health and social care for young people.

Rescuer/Villain to Coach/Challenger

It is all very well with young people, but what about when other professionals appear to be the issue? How can we interact in a way that shifts this dynamic?

A few years ago, I was supporting a young person who had a mental-health diagnosis which she disagreed with. She felt that her mental-health nurse did not understand her, and did not like her so she just stopped engaging with them. I could see her point—I thought the diagnosis did not sit right, and from what I gathered, the nurse was quite abrupt. I decided to ring this nurse and tell her that I thought the diagnosis needed reconsidering, and that I thought that the way they responded to this young person when they were struggling needed to be different. The nurse listened and then told me that they were the ones with the clinical knowledge and that I needed to follow their lead. This reinforced my resistance to them, which made it difficult for me to help the young person overcome the issues. Eventually, the nurse actually said that I was making things worse and asked me to stop working with the young person!

What did I do wrong? I made some assumptions. I assumed that the nurse and her team did not care, that they were inflexible and did not want to engage with what the young person needed for their emotional well-being. I came from a stance of telling them how to do their job. It is not surprising that I was quickly shut down and eventually excluded from the process.

How could I approach this differently to shift towards a more credible and empowering dynamic? I could start with building a shared goal with the nurse—'I'm a youth worker working with X, and I know they have been struggling. I wanted to touch base with you to see if there is anything I can do in my role as a youth worker to support what you are doing with them.' Hopefully, this opener has allowed the nurse to feel safe, not attacked; I have begun to build trust and collaboration. After listening to their response, I might say something like, 'X has mentioned to me that they feel their diagnosis might not be quite right and this impacts the way they are supported when they're in crisis. Could we have a conversation about this when convenient as I would like to better understand the rationale for the decisions that have been made?'

In this interaction, I would have left the door open for future collaboration, and after the further conversation I requested, I would be able to go back to the young person with useful knowledge. Their perception was that the nurse was being unfair, but there might be good reasons for the decisions being made. In this example, their diagnosis was wrong and was eventually changed, but blowing up my relationship with the nurse did not help anyone. I learned a lot from that situation!

By using trauma-informed and youth-work principles of empowerment, we can disrupt patterns of silo-working, ego-stroking, territory-protecting, defence-ready interactions. We can position ourselves as competent and credible partners with others seeking to help young people. Their roles, boundaries and ways of working may be different to ours, but we look for ways to bring out the best in situations together, for the good of the young person.

Shared Language, Shared Objectives

Traditionally, youth work and youth workers have been low down the food chain in relation to social workers, probation officers, nurses, teachers. The Drama Triangle gives us some insight into why this may happen, but it is not the whole story. The other issue, I believe, is a lack of shared language between youth workers and other professionals, especially clinical professionals. An understanding of trauma-informed youth work can address this.

It can be hard for other professionals to understand the important role that youth workers play, especially when youth workers are voluntary and unqualified. We even feel within ourselves that what we do is basic, obvious and simple, and that when young people are struggling we are quickly out of our depth and need to hand them over to specialists. I would argue that we need to value our contribution, and develop language around it that enables others to value it too. We may not have all the expertise of the professional but we can make the difference between that young person engaging with them, or rejecting their help.

It can be hard for other professionals to understand the role that youth workers play

As we become more confident in the validity of youth work, aware of ways to avoid drama and instead work collaboratively and in an empowering way with young people and other adults, understanding trauma-informed care allows us to translate that value into language that is familiar to other professionals.

As a youth worker, you do not just hang out with young people. You create a *safe* environment built on *trust* where young people can benefit from *peer support* and engage in activities which build their *resilience*. You do this from a *non-judgmental* stance, enabling young people to *build on their strengths* while equipping them to *overcome their challenges*. You can be confident in your role when speaking with their social worker or mental-health nurse (or whoever you are working alongside), working *collaboratively* with them for the best outcomes for the young person.

6 Informed and Equipped

When working with young people who have experienced, or are now experiencing trauma, it is helpful to be able to recognize and celebrate the glimmers of hope and healing that represent progress. Seeing some light enables us to have a sense of encouragement, indicating that we are actually helping in what can feel like a very long, dark tunnel. Most importantly, we can then reflect this back to the young person, helping them see that they are beginning to recover a sense of peace, some distance from the effects of trauma, and that hope and healing are possible and within reach.

The Three S's of Healing

The three S's of healing begin with what needs to happen on the inside, to allow a person to express themselves and regain a sense of connectedness with those around them.

Safety

The sense of safety needed for anyone struggling because of trauma must be first kindled inside of them before the outward expressions of it can be seen. This happens with the help of supportive others through co-regulation.

We can equip young people to notice a growing sense of safety by encouraging them to 'befriend their nervous system.'[17] After establishing a trusting relationship with the young person and enabling them to feel safe with us, we can equip young people to check in with themselves and notice when they feel safe, and when they do not. We can explore with them what helped them to feel safe and this can form a basis for finding that sense of safety at other times when we are not around. Noticing what that sense of safety feels like will also equip young people to be able to notice more quickly when they feel unsafe, and why.

For the young person, establishing that they feel safe in the presence of another person will allow them to recognize that this is a space where they feel emotionally supported, that they are understood. From this space, young people can be helped to think through who else in their life they feel supported and understood by, and who might be around when this sense vanishes.

Things to help young people look out for that signal this internal kindling of safety:

- Starting to think clearly
- Hands, arms and legs feeling more relaxed
- Breathing is slowing/becoming steady
- Concepts like fun and hope start to feel within reach (even if not fully grasped yet)

Self-expression

Once young people feel anchored internally and somewhat secure, they become more able to articulate what is going on for them, and what they need. We are often keen for young people to jump straight to this point and tell us what is wrong, but until the inner foundations are there, this will be very difficult. This is why trauma-informed youth work is so vital, as we can help young people settle through co-regulation which will enable them to engage in dialogue with others around them. We can equip young people to do this in ways that feel safe for them by suggesting tools that could help them.

For example, if a young person has a meeting with a mental-health professional where they want to discuss how they feel on bad days, we could suggest they draw a picture expressing this and take it with them to show the person and tell them about the different elements of it. If a young person wants to have a conversation with their parent about what does and does not help when they are feeling distressed, we could help them make a traffic-light list where they note down what they need when they are feeling green (all good), amber (not great but coping) or red (really not coping, need help).

In this way, we are building on the foundations of co-regulation, using youth-work principles to help the young person engage with others. We empower them to begin to work collaboratively with people in a position of authority rather than feeling done to. We are engaging in informal education which enables them to participate and have a voice into things that matter to them.

Synergy

As young people move further out of a trauma response, their capacity for empathy and emotional responsiveness to others comes back online. They become able to add to, and enhance the atmosphere within which they exist. This might look like:

- Noticing someone else's emotions and responding compassionately
- Feeling excited, joyful or enjoying a shared experience
- Regaining a sense of the positive difference they make to others around them

We can equip young people to do this by modelling it through our practice with them and their peers, and giving them safe spaces within which to practice. For example, we might do an activity with a group where we pass around a piece of paper for each person which has each individual's name on it and everyone writes something on it which they appreciate or think is great about that person. In this way, young people are able to give and receive positive feedback and get an insight into the value they have as a person within the peer group or community—the light they bring, to recall our theological reflection in chapter three. It is so liberating and exciting to be able to embrace this stage because, as we know, humans are wired for connection by a creator who reaches into our darkness and isolation, our stuck-ness, and lights the way back into relationship.

As we talk with young people, we can help them notice ways in which they have been able to come out of that very shut-down place that is so natural in trauma and see glimpses of connection. This will allow them to recognize the progress they are making and form a foundation for more. It will embolden them, and rekindle hope.

What About Us?

The principles above help us to recognize when our trauma-informed youth work is having a positive impact on young people, but the foundation is that we have a sense of peace and safety to lend young people. So how do we stay grounded, always able to embody the peace that young people need? How do we avoid being buffeted by the storms of our circumstances?

The short answer is that we do not. It is not possible, so do not set yourself up to fail by thinking you must! However, there are ways that we can equip ourselves in this respect, so that our work with young people can be a marathon, not a sprint, and so that our presence in their lives is, more often than not, one that contains contagious peace.

Aligned with the Truth

As Christians, we can have peace which is 'beyond understanding' (Phil 4.7), which means it is not dependent on our circumstances, but comes from our connection to God through the indwelling of the Holy Spirit.[18] We can think of it like a plumb line which comes down from heaven showing us the truth about who we are and who God is.

When we surrender ourselves to God, we put him in charge of our lives, and choose to bring ourselves under his authority. When we become part of his family, his Spirit causes us to become spiritually alive. In this way, God is truly our Father, the source of our spiritual life, and we are grafted in to his life by his Spirit. It is through this ongoing relationship that the Holy Spirit, in partnership with our spirit, guards our hearts and minds.

It can be so easy to do things without knowing why, finding ourselves caught in negative emotions that lead us to think things about ourselves which are not true. This can be so destabilizing, and it is all backwards, like the tail wagging the dog. That sense of empowerment which is so vital for young people is necessary for all of us—feeling like a victim, a slave to our circumstances and emotions is not the life we were created for.

When our heads and hearts are under the lordship of Jesus, through the Holy Spirit we can think thoughts and make decisions with his inspiration. We can be more anchored in our emotions, submitting them to him and not being ruled by them. This will then be expressed in our actions and our presence in the world.

Therefore, the first piece of equipment for us in this work is alignment with the Holy Spirit, who brings peace and shows us the truth about who we are and who God is.

Befriending Our Own Nervous System

Deb Dana speaks of befriending our nervous system, which might sound odd since it is an autonomic process—it does its thing automatically without us thinking about it, like our digestive system. But just like our digestion, we can be a friend or foe depending on our choices—as any lactose-intolerant person will attest! We can help our nervous system to experience and broadcast safety by developing a stance of compassion and forgiveness.[19]

Compassion allows us to realize that the person in front of us is 'just like me'

Compassion allows us to realize that the person in front of us is 'just like me.' It guards against tendencies towards being (even unintentionally) judgmental, perceiving the other person as bad or broken and needing to be fixed. Compassion reminds us that we too have experienced being hijacked by feelings of dysregulation, how distressing and disempowering this feels at the time, and the fact that it is possible to recover. This can help us if we feel threatened or out of our depth when faced with a situation where there is dysregulation, whether this is coming from a young person, a parent, a professional, even our boss! Every person, just like me, has a nervous system that experiences times of dysregulation, that senses danger and responds to protect itself. Just like me, they will be helped by picking up on a sense of calm and non-threatening presence from my nervous system. I do not need to be pulled into my own state of autonomic defence. I can stay open through a stance of compassion.

Dana goes on to say that forgiveness is tied to having a regulated nervous system. When we recall a memory from a place of unforgiveness, we experience the dysregulated feelings of anger, betrayal and shame that go along with it. This sends us back into a dysregulated state in the present and we may then interact with others out of this. However, when we forgive, we can acknowledge the issue, but do so from being anchored in a sense of safety which disrupts the anxiety that comes with unforgiveness. By keeping a stance of compassion and forgiveness, we can increasingly become people of peace. Dana is not religious, but it is uncanny how, once again, discoveries in neuroscience point to the life that Jesus models.

What might this look like in practice? Below are some questions to help you ground this in your own experience. It might be helpful to recall the Polyvagal Defence Hierarchy from chapter two, and the movement between the three pathways: connection, action and shutdown.

- What does it feel like for you to be grounded in a state of safety, peace and connection? Consider how your body feels, and what is going on in your mind and emotions. Practice purposely inhabiting that space and visualize peace being broadcast from you into your surroundings.
- Think of a time when you encountered a person or situation where you had an inkling that there was a problem even though no one told you; you just sensed that things were not okay. What were the cues for this in your body, mind and emotions, in your spirit—how did you recognize it?
- Do you find you are susceptible to picking up on unspoken senses of anxiety, (broadcasts of danger) and being triggered into your own defence response? How might you become more able to distinguish between what is someone else's broadcast, and what is your own? It might be helpful to consider whether the sense of dis-ease came out of the blue, when entering a room, when a topic of conversation came up etc.
- How can the principles of empowerment help you guard against being in a drama triangle, or defaulting to defensiveness in conversations with authority figures or dependence with young people?
- At times when you feel dysregulated, threatened or out of your depth, what helps you to return to a place of peace where you can be on a firm foundation in terms of your own identity, your role and remit, your capacity to contribute; to hold hope for someone?

- What is the role of the Holy Spirit in your life in maintaining equilibrium and equipping you to bring peace to young people? How might you develop this?
- Picture someone whose presence or responses you often find challenging. Connect with how this impacts your emotions, thoughts and sensations within your body. Then bring in the awareness of compassion, that just like me, this person has a nervous system which is trying to cope and protect itself, to regulate. Ask God to show you this person through his perspective. Notice what changes for you in your thoughts, emotions and body as you do this. How might this open the door for forgiveness and a new capacity for connection?
- Ask God to show you how he sees you as a light-bringer. What does your light look like and what can it do? This might be something it would be helpful to recall at times when his light is particularly needed as you work with young people.

Conclusion

As our prince of peace, Jesus came into his world to make it possible for us to come back into relationship with him, to share in his light and life—to be the people he created us to be. Through disciplines like neuroscience and theology, we can begin to discover and unravel the mysteries of the way God created us as individuals, and his intentions for the way we co-exist together in community with each other and with him. While we can use all sorts of different language and ideas to understand and describe this, at the heart of it is this: as a person empowered by God's Spirit, you carry his contagious peace. This is much needed in the world…in fact, Jesus invites you to partner with him in 'changing the world—one nervous system at a time'![20]

Notes

1 Polyvagal Defence Hierarchy: Porges, Sanders, Hoskin, Levine: https://equusoma.com/wp-content/uploads/2020/04/Polyvagal-Defense-Hierarchy-A4.pdf

2 D Dana, *Anchored: How to Befriend Your Nervous System Using Polyvagal Theory* (London: Vermilion, 2021).

3 D Dana, *The Polyvagal Theory in Therapy: Engaging the Rhythm of Regulation* (New York: W W Norton and Company, 2018) pp 211–215.

4 https://www.hoffmaninstitute.co.uk/trauma-resilience-and-addiction-hoffman-interviews-dr-gabor-mate/

5 D Dana, *Anchored*, *op cit*, p 176.

6 M Scott, J Dunn and J Rogerson, *Eerdmans Commentary on the Bible: John* (Grand Rapids, MI: Eerdmans, 2021).

7 'There's a Massive Gap between the Number of Young People Referred to CAMHS and the Number of Doctors Who Can See Them,' https://www.youthscape.co.uk/research/translating-god/theres-a-massive-gap-between-the-number-of-young-people-referred-to-camhs-and-the-number-of-doctors-who-can-see-them

8 L Christie and D Nystrom, *A Youth Worker's Commentary on John* (Grand Rapids, MI: Zondervan, 2011) p 34.

9 J Swinton, *Spirituality and Mental Health Care* (London: Jessica Kingsley Publishers, 2001) p 140 (my emphases).

10 D Da Silva, *Shifting Atmospheres* (Shippensburg, PA: Destiny Image Publishers 2017) p 130.

11 *ibid*, p 135.

12 D Dana, *Anchored*, *op cit*, p 176.

13 G Bright, *Youth Work: Histories, Policy and Contexts* (London: Bloomsbury Academic, 2015) p 2.

14 T Jeffs and M K Smith, 'Introducing Youth Work,' in J Jeffs and M K Smith (eds), *Youth Work Practice* (Basingstoke: Palgrave Macmillan, 2010) p 3.

15 https://nya.org.uk/national-youth-work-curriculum/

16 S Karpman, 'The New Drama Triangles,' 2007: https://karpmandramatriangle.com/pdf/thenewdramatriangles.pdf, 1.

17 D Dana, *Anchored*, *op cit*,

18 B Roberts Gaventa *et al*, *Eerdmans Commentary on the Bible: Galatians and Philippians* (Grand Rapids, MI: Eerdmans, 2021).

19 D Dana, *Anchored*, *op cit*, pp 142–144.

20 D Dana, *Anchored*, *op cit*, p 176.